Spooky Spots

SPOOKY CASTLES

MEGAN BORGERT-SPANIOL

Big Buddy Books

An Imprint of Abdo Publishing
abdobooks.com

abdobooks.com

Published by Abdo Publishing, a division of ABDO, PO Box 398166, Minneapolis, Minnesota 55439.

Printed in the United States of America, North Mankato, Minnesota
052020
092020

Design: Sarah DeYoung, Mighty Media, Inc.
Production: Mighty Media, Inc.
Editor: Liz Salzmann

Cover Photograph: Shutterstock Images
Interior Photographs: Fvengoechea/Wikimedia Commons, pp. 6 (Alboraya), 9; Lukáš Kalista/Wikimedia Commons, p. 19; Shutterstock Images, pp. 4–5, 6, 7 (all), 10, 11, 13, 15, 16–17, 21, 23, 24–25, 27, 28 (all), 29 (all)
Design Elements: Shutterstock Images

Library of Congress Control Number: 2020931736

Publisher's Cataloging-in-Publication Data
Names: Borgert-Spaniol, Megan, author.
Title: Spooky castles / by Megan Borgert-Spaniol
Description: Minneapolis, Minnesota : Abdo Publishing, 2021 | Series: Spooky spots | Includes online resources and index
Identifiers: ISBN 9781532193309 (lib. bdg.) | ISBN 9781098211943 (ebook)
Subjects: LCSH: Haunted places--Juvenile literature. | Ghosts--Juvenile literature. | Castles--Juvenile literature. | Spirits--Juvenile literature.
Classification: DDC 133.12--dc23

CONTENTS

HAUNTED CASTLES

Do you believe there are ghosts among us? Many people do. Whether you're a believer or not, castles are some of the spookiest spots around!

Get ready to **explore** some of the most haunted castles on Earth. Climb to the top of a castle tower. Feel the chill inside an old **dungeon**. But look out! You may not be alone.

Castles are even spookier at night!

World's Spookiest CASTLES

Are you ready for a ghostly adventure? Then pack up your wits and your **courage**. Let's take a trip to some of the world's spookiest castles!

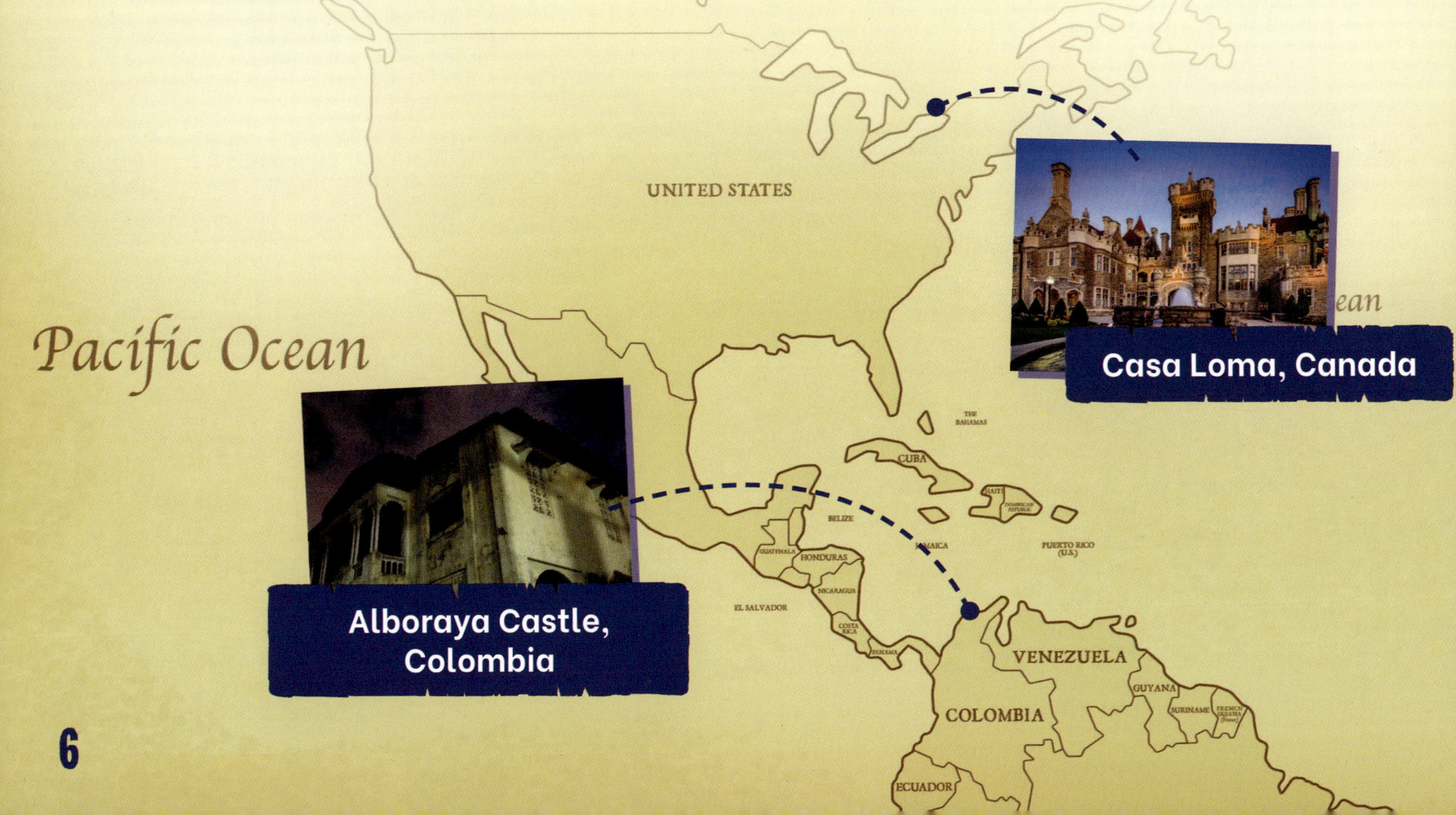

Leap Castle, Ireland
Houska Castle, Czech Republic
Moosham Castle, Austria
Himeji Castle, Japan
Castle of Good Hope, South Africa
N
E
S
W
GERMANY
POLAND
BELARUS
UKRAINE
FRANCE
ITALY
ROMANIA
SPAIN
PORTUGAL
MONGOLIA
CHINA
INDIA
JAPAN
MOROCCO
ALGERIA
LIBYA
MAURITANIA
MALI
NIGER
NIGERIA
GUINEA
ETHIOPIA
SOMALIA
KENYA
TANZANIA
ANGOLA
NAMIBIA
BOTSWANA
ZIMBABWE
SOUTH AFRICA
DEMOCRATIC REPUBLIC OF THE CONGO
AFGHANISTAN
PAKISTAN
Ocean
AUSTRALIA

ALBORAYA CASTLE

Alboraya Castle was built in Colombia in 1626. It was owned by a man called Rondón. **Legend** has it that Rondón **threatened** anyone who came near his land. To guard his property, he rode a black horse smeared with human blood.

To this day, people nearby say they hear a horse running through the streets in the middle of the night. Some have also reported hearing a woman cry out. People who go to the castle report a feeling of being watched.

In Spanish, Alboraya Castle is known as *Castillo de la Alboraya*.

MOOSHAM CASTLE

Austria's Moosham Castle is more than 800 years old. In the 1600s, it was host to witch **trials**.

During these trials, thousands of people were **accused** of witchcraft. Many of them were **tortured** and killed. Their spirits are believed to haunt the castle's halls and grounds.

FRIGHTFUL FACT

A total of 139 people were killed during the witch trials at Moosham. Most of them were poor, male, and between the ages of 10 and 21.

Moosham Castle sits 3,540 feet (1,079 m) above sea level.

In the 1800s, deer and cattle around the castle started suddenly dying. Some locals thought the animal deaths were caused by **werewolves**.

People living in the castle were **accused** of being werewolves. Many of these people were put to death.

Today, castle visitors report seeing and feeling the presence of ghosts. Reports also include hearing banging sounds and footsteps, and seeing white mists.

Ghost hunters call white mist "ecto-mist." They say this is a form ghosts often take.

CASTLE OF GOOD HOPE

The Castle of Good Hope is a former military **fortress** in South Africa. It was built in the 1600s. Prisoners were held in a **dungeon** there. They were chained to the walls and **tortured**.

Legend says these prisoners haunt the fortress. Visitors have heard voices and footsteps. The fortress may also be haunted by a soldier who hung himself in the bell tower. Some people say the bell rings by itself!

FRIGHTFUL FACT

The Castle of Good Hope is said to be home to a ghost dog! A large black dog has been reported to leap at visitors before disappearing.

The Castle of Good Hope is on the Atlantic coast. At high tide, the castle dungeon would sometimes flood and prisoners would drown.

HOUSKA CASTLE

The Czech Republic's Houska Castle dates back to the 1200s. It is said to be built around a bottomless hole in the ground.

Some believe this hole is the gateway to the underworld. According to **legend**, the castle was built to keep **demons** from entering our world.

FRIGHTFUL FACT

It is said that strange beings have come out of the hole. These include spooky flying creatures and animal-human hybrids.

Houska Castle lies about 30 miles (48 km) north of Prague, the capital of the Czech Republic.

One spooky tale tells of a prisoner who was lowered into the hole. After a moment of silence, the prisoner started screaming. When he was pulled out, he had white hair and wrinkles. He looked like he had aged 30 years!

Today, people report seeing **demons** flying around the grounds of the castle. A woman in white has also been spotted looking out of a castle window.

The chapel of Houska Castle is said to be built over the "Gateway to Hell."

CASA LOMA

Casa Loma is a Canadian castle built in 1914. Sir Henry Pellatt and his wife, Lady Mary, lived there. When the couple lost most of their wealth, they had to leave the castle. But some say their ghosts returned to Casa Loma!

Workers at the castle have reported sightings of Sir Henry and Lady Mary. Some have felt as though their hair was being pulled. Visitors have even recorded the voice of a male spirit!

FRIGHTFUL FACT

A film crew once tried to make a movie in Lady Mary's room. But the camera seemed to shut off on its own. Some thought Lady Mary was trying to stop the filming!

A ghost called "The White Lady" is said to live at Casa Loma. She is believed to have worked as a maid at the castle.

LEAP CASTLE

Ireland's Leap Castle has a dark history. In the 1500s, a **priest** was murdered by his brother in a **chapel** in the castle. The chapel became known as the Bloody Chapel. It is said to be haunted by the priest's ghost.

In the 1600s, another death took place. A girl named Emily is said to have fallen from the castle's highest tower. Some say her ghost can be seen reenacting her fall.

FRIGHTFUL FACT

Leap Castle has been featured on four different television shows about haunted places.

Leap Castle was home to the O'Carroll clan. This clan was known for being mean and scary.

The **legend** of Leap Castle only gets darker. Workers at the castle are said to have removed human bones from a **dungeon** in the castle.

The dungeon had **spikes** sticking up from the floor. It is believed prisoners were dropped onto the spikes. There, they died slow and painful deaths.

With its history of death, Leap Castle is full of **paranormal** activity. Visitors have reported a sheeplike spirit that smells of rotten eggs. There are also reports of a "Red Lady" carrying a big knife!

Today, the owners of Leap Castle report regular paranormal activity. But they don't mind being surrounded by spirits.

HIMEJI CASTLE

Himeji Castle was built in Japan in the 1300s. It carries the haunting **legend** of Okiku. Okiku was the servant of a **samurai** who lived in the castle. The samurai wrongfully **accused** Okiku of losing one of his ten golden plates.

The samurai killed Okiku by throwing her down a well. After her death, Okiku's ghost was said to crawl from the well to **torment** her killer. Some say her ghost still haunts the castle at night!

FRIGHTFUL FACT

The 2002 horror movie *The Ring* was based on the legend of Okiku.

Himeji Castle is also known as White Heron Castle.

SPOOKY OR SCIENCE?

You've just learned about some spooky castles. The creepy stories are fun! But good **explorers** look for reasons for what they see and hear. Strange happenings can often be explained by science.

Do you think the castles in this book are actually haunted? You might have to visit them to find out!

IMAGINATION

Humans have excellent imaginations. Just hearing about a scary sight can trick your brain into thinking you've seen it too!

NOISES OR VOICES

Cameras and recorders can pick up all kinds of odd sounds. Some of these sounds can be mistaken as voices. With recordings, it's easy to hear what we want to hear!

EXAGGERATION

Tourist sites may **exaggerate** spooky stories. They hope this will make more people want to visit.

INFRASOUND

Infrasound is a sound that is too low for humans to hear. But we can still sense it. Studies have shown infrasound can make people feel uncomfortable. It can even cause us to see or hear things that aren't actually there.

GLOSSARY

accuse – to say someone did something wrong or illegal.

chapel – a small church, usually connected to a larger church or other building.

courage – strength or bravery.

demon – an evil spirit.

dungeon – a prison or cell, usually underground.

exaggerate (ihg-ZA-juh-rayt) – to make something seem larger or more impressive.

explore – to go into in order to make a discovery or to have an adventure. A person who explores is an explorer.

fortress – a building or town with strong walls to guard against enemies.

hybrid – a mix of two or more things.

legend – an old story that many people believe but cannot be proven true.

paranormal – unable to be explained by science.

priest – an important member in some Christian churches.

samurai – a Japanese warrior who lived hundreds of years ago.

spike – something long and pointed like a nail.

threaten – to say that you will harm someone or something.

torment – to cause pain or suffering.

torture – to purposely cause great pain and suffering to someone.

tourist site – a place people visit while on vacation.

trial – a meeting before a judge to find out whether someone did something wrong or illegal.

werewolf – a person who can take the form of a wolf.

ONLINE RESOURCES

To learn more about spooky castles, please visit **abdobooklinks.com** or scan this QR code. These links are routinely monitored and updated to provide the most current information available.

INDEX